Thoughts for a day

Part One   MORNING   *page 5*

Part Two   AFTERNOON   *19*

Part Three   EVENING   *37*

This anthology was compiled by
the Reverend David Matheson Hunter BD AKC
in the last year of his life and is published
as a memorial by his widow, Hilary.

David studied theology at King's College, London, and was ordained in Exeter Cathedral in 1976. After serving curacies in Paignton and Plymstock, Devon, he was appointed Chaplain at the Anglican Cathedral of St George in Jerusalem. On return to England he became Rector of the Benefice of Brinkley, Burrough Green, Westley Waterless and Carlton, near Newmarket, Suffolk, later becoming Rector of the Benefice of Bressingham, Fersfield and the Lophams, near Diss, Norfolk. In 1996 David semi-retired to become Chaplain to Wymondham Abbey, Norfolk, finally having to fully retire in 2001.

Compilation © David Hunter
Icon drawings (of Russian origin, 15th - 16th c) © Helen McIldowie-Jenkins

ISBN 0 900616 73 3
Printed and Published 14 October 2005
by Geo. R Reeve Ltd, 9-11 Town Green,
Wymondham, Norfolk NR18 0BD
Telephone 01953 602297

Preface

'A Day' is a measurement of time, but it carries a huge freight of meaning in religious and poetic imagery. We only have one word in English for time, but the Greek language had two, *chronos* and *kairos*. *Chronos* measures time but *kairos* means 'due season', 'right time', 'occasion to act', etc.

Chronos answers the question 'What time is it?'
Kairos answers the question 'What is time for?'

Time is for God and He gives us the time so that we might draw closer to Him and find the secret of eternal life.

This little anthology, divided up into three parts of the day, is a medley of poetry, prayers and prose from authors who have helped to inspire me during the twenty-five years of my parochial ministry.

Ascensiontide 2004

The Reverend David Hunter

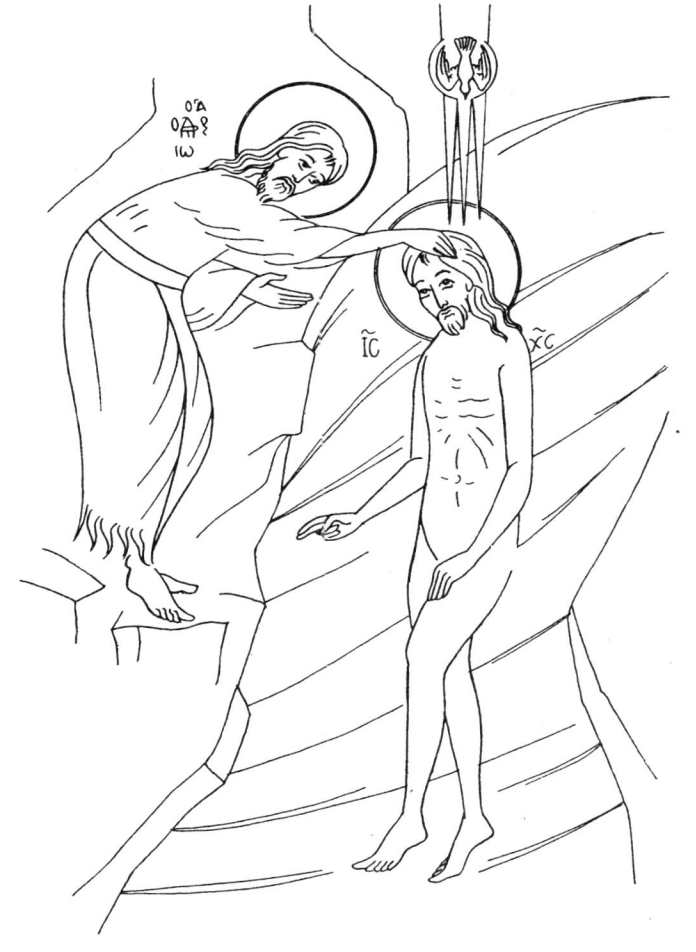

Part One
MORNING

'Thou makest new those born on Earth' (J. Baggley, *Festival Icons for the Christian Year,* Compline of the Feast of the Theophany, Canticle 5)

Baptism - symbolising Renewal in the Spirit

We have to live but one day at a time,
                         but we are living for eternity in that one day.

Anon

ON WAKING

Another day of wonder
Thou givest, O Lord,
In which to learn, to love,
To do well, and be glad.
Lord, let me find Thee in all things today;
Be Thou my Endless Day.

Thy light touches creation all around
With a brightness from heaven:
In the light of its joy our hearts leap;
In the light of Thy love our eyes see;
In the light of the glory of Thy grace
Let me learn and love, do well and be glad.

For this environment of the divine,
For this peep into glory,
For the new births of a new day,
Let me be glad and rejoice,
Let me give thanks, O my Endless, Only Day,
Today, all day, always.

Eric Milner-White from 'My God, My Glory'

THE LORD OF THE DANCE

The whole creation is dancing; the whole universe - galaxies, nebulae, stars and their satellites - is engaged in the great dance. They turn and come together, and draw apart, and come together again and so it has ever been, and so it shall be throughout all eternity.

Creation makes its own music. There is no created being that does not sing, and the music of everything that is joins together to make the great harmony and rhythm of the dance. Everything that exists treads the same measure, each according to its own rhythm, and every individual rhythm is related to, and is an integral part of, the rhythm of the dance.

These rhythms are reflected in the life-cycle of beings, and there is no part of creation which does not have its own life-cycle, whether they be creatures of a day, like some insects, or plants, or trees, or men, the rocks and the rivers, and earth itself, and indeed the whole universe as it is known to man. But man cannot conceive the joy of this rhythm as it truly is; he knows only its sorrowful face as he experiences it in a fallen world. He cannot know anything of creation as creation truly is. He can only with difficulty recognise the rhythm of the universe, and only haltingly and supported on all sides can he attempt to tread its measure. He cannot know this universe of which he is a part, and the explorations of his intellect, and the discoveries of his science can only lead him into a greater bewilderment.

Anthony Duncan

The Clockmakers of old were astronomers and mathematicians. Time to them was not fretted down to when a train left the station or an office opened. They geared it to eternity, and harnessed time to the spheres. Some of their timepieces act as perpetual almanacs, for they tell not only what o'clock it is but which day of the month and reveal the movement of the heavenly bodies throughout the year.

The church clock in West Acre Norfolk has, instead of the hours on its dial, the twelve letters WATCH AND PRAY. There is a clock still working which chimes a carillon of eight bells: all the week it plays secular tunes but on Sunday morning only, it plays 'O Worship the King'.

It is the disciple or apostle clock that interests us most. None seems to have been made in this country and they are rare anywhere. Having been wrought by hand, no two are identical, but they all have more or less the same principle. Christ is shown enthroned among the heavenly bodies. When twelve strikes, a door opens in the clock and from an inner chamber twelve figures, representing the twelve apostles, troop forth and pass the figure of Christ. Each bow to his Master as he passes, except the last, Judas, who turns away from him, while Christ, with upraised arm, blesses each before he disappears.

A Gaelic proverb tells us that prayer is the key of the day, and the lock of the night. There are twelve apostles and twelve hours of the day and night. A disciple, therefore, for each hour, ceaselessly keeping watch and ward round the clock, always on time because they are of the very substance of time, without beginning or end, ever present.

The old clockmakers were wise to gear their timepieces to eternity and harness them to the spheres. For they knew that it is by heart beats, not by mechanical ticks, that our lives are measured; that though death was sure, it could not snap the mainspring when man shared with God what can never be encompassed by the wheeling finger of time. They had learnt that eternity resides not in the puff of a child's breath blowing at a dandelion top, but within the child.

N Brysson Morrison from 'The Keeper of Time'

It is the wanderer, the life-explorer, who is the true naturalist, collecting experiences and making maps for spiritual eyes. What then does he note? First, the knowledge of beauty. Something in the soul suddenly rises up and cries 'yes' to something that makes him aware that he is looking at beauty.

As he gazes, he knows himself in communion with what he sees. Thus, looking at the opening of dawn over the sea, he is filled with gladness, his spirits rising with the sun. He wishes to shout and sing. He is one with the birds that have begun singing, and all wild nature waking refreshed after the night. But looking out at evening of the same day over the grey sea he is filled with unutterable sorrow. I looked out at all the strange beauty and felt all the desolateness of the world, all the exiledom of man upon it. It was as if a sad minstrel sat before me and played unendingly the story of a lost throne, a lost family, a lost world.

Then a thought came to me: 'We are all the children of kings; on our spiritual bodies are royal seals. Sometime or other we were abandoned on this beautiful garden, the world. We expected someone to return for us, but no-one came. We lived on, and to forget homesickness devised means of pleasure, games, occupations. We have entirely forgotten the lost heritage and the mystery of our abandonment; we have forgotten the great mystery of life.' It is our religion to remember, to count nothing as important beside the initial mystery. What is beauty is every little experience that reminds us of our mystery.

Stephen Graham from 'A Tramp's Sketches'

I have only just a minute,
Only sixty seconds in it.
Forced upon me -
Can't refuse it.
But it's up to me to use it.
I must suffer if I lose it.
Give account if I abuse it.
Just a tiny little minute,
But eternity is in it.

Anon

YOUTH

Youth is not a time of life, it is a state of mind. It is not a matter of ripe cheeks, red lips and supple knees.

It is -
- A temper of the will
- A quality of the imagination
- A vigour of the emotions
- A freshness of the deep springs of life.

Youth means a temperamental predominance of courage over timidity, of the appetite of adventure over love of ease. This often exists in a man over fifty more than a boy of twenty; nobody grows old by merely living a number of years; people grow old by deserting their ideals.

Years wrinkle the skin, but to give up enthusiasm wrinkles the soul.

Worry, doubt, self distrust, fear and despair, these are the long, long years that bow the head and turn the growing spirit back into dust.

Whether seventy or seventeen, there is in every being's heart the love of wonder, the sweet amazement of the stars, the undaunted challenge of events, the unfailing child-like appetite for what next, and the joy and the game of life.

You are -
>   As young as your faith - as old as your doubt.
>   As young as your self-confidence - as old as your fear.
>   As young as your hope - as old as your despair.

In the central place of your heart there is a wireless station; so long as it receives messages of beauty, hope, cheer, courage, grandeur and power from the earth and from the infinite, so long are you young.

When the wires are all down and the central place of your heart is covered with snows of pessimism and the ice of cynicism, then you are grown old indeed; and may God have mercy on your soul.

Paul H Duhn

No man ever sank under the burden of the day. It is when tomorrow's burden is added to the burden of today that the weight is more than he can bear. If you find yourself so loaded, remember this: it is your own doing, not God's. He begs you to leave the future to Him, and mind the present.

George MacDonald

A LITTLE WAY OF PRAYER

Let us, by an act of the will, place ourselves in the presence of our Divine Lord, and with an act of faith, ask that He will empty us of self and ALL desire save that His Most Blessed Will may be done, and that it illumine our hearts and minds. We can then gather together all those for whom our prayers have been asked, and hold them silently up to Him, making no special request - neither asking nor beseeching - but just resting, with them, IN Him, desiring nothing but that Our Lord may be glorified in them.

In this most simple way of approach He does make known His Most Blessed Will for us. 'For so He giveth Himself to His beloved in quietness'.

Dorothy Kerin from 'Chapel House Notes'

I bind unto myself today
The power of God to hold and lead,
His eye to watch, His might to stay,
His ear to hearken to my need,
The wisdom of my God to teach,
His hand to guide, His shield to ward,
The Word of God to give me speech,
His heavenly host to be my guard.

Cecil Alex from 'Saint Patrick's Breastplate'

Part Two
AFTERNOON

'His face shone like the Sun'
(Matthew 17.2)

Transfiguration - symbolising Christ's divinity and spiritual light in our physical world.

Love all God's Creation,
The whole world and every grain of sand.
Love every leaf and every ray of God's light.
Love animals and plants.
Love everything.
But remember that you must face the mystery of God in everything you love.

Dostoevsky

THE DIVINE WEAVER

My life is but a weaving
Between my Lord and me;
I cannot choose the colours
He worketh steadily.

Oftentimes he weaveth sorrow
And I, in foolish pride,
Forget that he seeth the upper,
And I the under side.

Not till the loom is silent
And the shuttles cease to fly,
Shall God unroll the canvas
And explain the reason why.

The dark threads are as needful
In the weaver's skilful hand
As the threads of gold and silver
In the pattern he has planned.

Anon

Dear God,

We give thanks for places of simplicity and peace. Let us find such a place within ourselves. We give thanks for places of refuge and beauty. Let us find such a place within ourselves. We give thanks for places of nature's truth and freedoms of joy, inspiration and renewal, places where all creatures may find acceptance and belonging. Let us search for these places; in a world, in ourselves and in others. Let us restore them. Let us strengthen and protect them and let us create them.

May we mend this outer world according to the truth of our inner life and may our souls be shaped and nourished by nature's eternal wisdom.

Amen.

Michael Leunig from 'A Common Prayer'

If there is righteousness in the heart, there will be beauty in the character.
If there be beauty in the character, there is harmony in the home.
If there is harmony in the home, there will be order in the nation.
When there is order in the nation, there will be peace in the world.

Chinese Proverb - Anon

Does not today's art reflect a world in crisis, deprived of security and truth?

Despite a profusion without precedent of media at his disposal, modern man experiences a growing difficulty to meet or encounter his neighbour, whose face he so often does not even notice. As fast as the human face, above all its nobility, has disappeared from contemporary art, its opposite - the beast - has substituted itself in a strange way...... The light of our world transformed into a gigantic garbage can, offered as 'art'. Should we not admit that our present rationalistic and technical exclusiveness is being paid for with a perilous atrophy of our general faculties?

'When souls start to break down, then faces also degenerate' wrote the Russian author Nicholas Gogol.

Michael Quenot from 'The Icon'

To be a Christian means to forgive the inexcusable, because God has forgiven the inexcusable in you.

C S Lewis

Once in a saintly passion I cried in wretched grief,
'O Lord, I am disgraceful, of sinners I am the chief.'
Then came my guardian angel, and standing right behind, said,
'Vanity, my little man, you're nothing of the kind!'

James B V Thomson

NOT ALL THERE

I turned to speak to God
About the world's despair;
But to make matters worse
I found God wasn't there.

God turned to speak to me.
(Don't everybody laugh)
God found I wasn't there -
At least not over half.

from 'The Poetry of Robert Frost'

'Men will carry guns until they learn to carry the Cross.'

Anon

CHRIST AND THE SOLDIER

The straggled soldier halted - stared at Him -
Then clumsily dumped down upon his knees,
Gasping, 'O blessed crucifix, I'm beat!'
And Christ, still sentried by the seraphim,
Near the front-line, between two splintered trees,
Spoke to him: 'My son, behold these hands and feet.'

The soldier eyed Him upward, limb by limb,
Paused at the Face; then muttered, 'Wounds like these
Would shift a bloke to Blighty just a treat!'
Christ, gazing downward, grieving and ungrim,
Whispered, 'I made for you the mysteries,
Beyond all battles moves the Paraclete.'

The soldier chucked his rifle in the dust,
And slipped his pack, and wiped his neck, and said -
'O Christ Almighty, stop this bleeding fight!'
Above that hill the sky was stained like rust
With smoke. In sullen daybreak flashing red
The guns were thundering bombardments blight.

The soldier cried 'I was born full of lust,
With hunger, thirst, and wishfulness to wed.
Who cares today if I done wrong or right?'
Christ asked all pitying, 'Can you put no trust
In my known word that shrives each faithful head?
Am I not resurrection, life and light?'

Siegfried Sassoon from 'War Poems'

Dear God

We loosen our grip.
We open our hand.
We are accepting.
In our empty hand we feel the shape of simple eternity.
It nestles there, we hold it gently.
We are accepting.

Michael Leunig from 'A Common Prayer'

He who has found his soul's life in God is happy, not in a truth with perfect happiness, but a foretaste thereof. He has a secret joy which is beyond the realms of temptation, unrest and sorrow, a quiet confidence and steadfastness which abide even while the waves and storms of life sweep over him.

God has promised not that he shall be free of crosses, rather do they form the ladder by which the soul mounts upwards, but that He will abide with his faithful servant through them all, and be his rock, his castle, his strong foundation.

Anon

One trouble with the churches is that too many people want to have Easter without Calvary.

Laurence Jacks

From Dust I rise
And out of Nothing now awake;
These Brighter Regions which salute mine Eyes
A Gift from God I take:
The Earth, the Seas, the Light, the lofty Skies,
The Sun and Stars are mine, if these I prize.

A Stranger here,
Strange things doth meet, strange Glory see,
Strange Treasures lodg'd in this fair World appear,
Strange all and New to me:
But that they mine should be who Nothing was,
That Strangest is of all; yet brought to pass.

Thomas Traherne from 'The Salutation'

Time and the bell have buried the day,
The black cloud carries the sun away.
Will the sunflower turn to us, will the clematis
Stray down, bend to us; tendril and spray
Clutch and cling?
Chill
Fingers of yew be curled
Down on us? After the kingfisher's wing
Has answered light to light, and is silent, the light is still
At the still point of the turning world.

T S Eliot from 'Four Quartets: Burnt Norton IV'

Part Three
EVENING

'Thou did lead us out of darkness'
(Adapted from Psalm 107.16)

Resurrection - symbolising
Salvation and freedom from fear
of the eternal night of oblivion.

Time goes, you say? Ah no!
Alas, Time stays, <u>we</u> go.

H A Dobson

Good Lord, yesterday is gone, tomorrow not yet come. This is today, and thou art in it, for Thou art the 'I am', the One that Is, and Thou art true to Thyself, yesterday, today and tomorrow. What Thou hast been, Thou wilt be: What thou wilt be, Thou art. Therefore I do not need to wait until tomorrow to know Thy saving health.

If my body aches, or breathing is hard, or nerves are strained, I do not need to wait and wonder if Thou wilt come to help me, for Thou hast said 'Now is the day of salvation'. So now I lean on that promise; now I surrender my troubles to Thee; now I accept Thy Salvation. Thou art with me and I am at peace.

Amen.

William Portsmouth from 'Healing Prayer'

Praised be my Lord for all who pardon one another for love's sake, and who endure weakness and tribulations; blessed are they who peacefully shall endure, for Thou, O Most High, will give them a crown.

Saint Francis of Assisi

The wounded surgeon plies the steel
That questions the distempered part;
Beneath the bleeding hands we feel
The sharp compassion of the healer's art
Resolving the enigma of the fever chart.

Our only health is the disease
If we obey the dying nurse
Whose constant care is not to please
But to remind of our, and Adam's curse,
And that, to be restored, our sickness must grow worse.

The whole earth is our hospital
Endowed by the ruined millionaire,
Wherein, if we do well, we shall
Die of the absolute paternal care
That will not leave us, but prevents us everywhere.

The dripping blood our only drink
The bloody flesh our only food:
In spite of which we like to think
That we are sound, substantial flesh and blood -
Again, in spite of that we call this Friday good.

T S Eliot from 'Four Quartets: East Coker IV'

God does not die on the day when we cease to believe in a personal deity; but we die on the day when our lives cease to be illuminated by the steady radiance renewed daily, of a wonder, the source of which is beyond all reason.

Dag Hammarskjold from 'Markings'

Let nothing disturb you;
let nothing frighten you;
all things pass,
God never changes.
Patience achieves all that it strives for.
He who has God
finds he lacks nothing.
God only meets all his needs.

St Teresa of Avila

The Resurrection cannot be tamed or tethered. It is a vast watershed in history, or it is nothing. It cannot be tested for truth; it is the test of lesser truths. No light can be thrown on it; its own light blinds the investigator. It does not compel belief; it resists it. But once accepted as fact, it tells more about the universe, about history, and about man's fate and state than all the mountains of other facts in the human accumulation.

Editorial in 'Life' magazine, 1956

Life itself is resurrection, or else it isn't life. We usually say that life is for living, but that's too fast. People who try to live by such an undigested maxim find themselves at a loss to deal with the only thing in life that is guaranteed to happen. They spend most of their days trying to run foul of death.

But death is not an inexplicable accident that happens to life; it is the very engine by which life runs. It is by the death of chickens, chicory and chickpeas that you have lived until today. Find even the life you now have is a perpetual dying: not only do all your tissues die and rise every seven years; your loves and your labours do too - frequently much faster than that, and for reasons good as well as bad. You cannot do the same job twice in a row without dying a little to the way you did it for the first time; and you certainly cannot love the same child - or man or woman - two days running unless you are willing to carry Monday's death with you into Tuesday's resurrection.

For to live is always to be rising from the dead. To reject death is to reject the only possible soil out of which life can come. That is a universal truth. Indeed, all that Christianity has added to it is an underscoring of its universality. Jesus did not superimpose some odd, additional truth. He simply assured us, by his death and resurrection, that even the one apparent exception to the process turns out to be another proof of the rule.

Robert Capon from 'The Supper of the Lamb'

WHEN I MEET GOD

In the castle of my soul there is a little postern gate, where,
When I enter, I am in the presence of God.
In a moment, in a turning of a thought,
I am where God is.

When I meet God there, all life gains a new meaning,
Small things become great, and great things small, lowly and despised things
Are shot through with glory.
My troubles seem but pebbles on the road,
My joys seem like the everlasting hills,
All my fever is gone in the peace of God
And I pass through the door from Time to Eternity.

Walter Rauschenbusch from 'The Little Gate to God'

God has great compassion on our weakness and great consideration for our littleness. The last thing he wants to do is to crush us. If he allows us to be broken when we are already down, worn out by our infirmities, it is in order that we may learn confidence...know with absolute certainty that each blow is really a mark of His love. That is the truth. I swear it!

Rejoice to think that after having recovered yourself in the midst of intense pain and difficulty, you will be able to help others in their turn. No one can help save he who has suffered. God destines you for this. Let this be your joy.

Abbé de Tourville

TIME'S PACES

When as a child I laughed and wept, Time CREPT.
When as a youth I waxed more bold, Time STROLLED.
When I became a full-grown man, Time RAN.
When older still I daily grew, Time FLEW.
Soon I shall find, in passing on, Time GONE.
O Christ! Wilt Thou have saved me then?
                                    Amen.

Canon Henry Twells (on a clock case in Chester Cathedral)

He who bends to himself a joy
Doth the wingèd life destroy;
But he who kisses the Joy as it flies
Lives in Eternity's sunrise.

William Blake from 'Eternity'

Seek not to have that everything should happen as you wish, but wish for everything to happen as it actually does happen, and you will be serene.

Epictetus

THANKSGIVING

I thank thee God that I have lived
In this great world and known its many joys;
The song of birds, the strong sweet smell of hay,
The cooling breezes in the secret dusk,
The flaming sunsets at the close of day,
Hills, and the lovely heather-covered moors,
Music at night, and moonlight on the sea,
The beat of waves upon the rocky shore
And wild white spray, flung in wild ecstasy;
The faithful eyes of dogs and treasured books,
The love of kin and fellowship of friends,
And all that makes life dear and beautiful.

I thank thee too, that I have known
A little sorrow and sometimes defeat,

A little heartache, and the loneliness
That comes from parting, and the word 'Goodbye':
Dawn breaking after dreary hours of pain,
When I discovered that night's gloom must yield
And morning light break through to me again.
Because of these and other blessings poured
Unasked upon my floundering head;
Because I know that there is yet to come
An even richer and more glorious life,
But most of all, because thine only Son
Once sacrificed life's loveliness for me,

I thank thee God that I have lived.

Anon (found among the offerings in a collection plate)

Being diminished by God means very often letting go whatever we are holding to become open handed for his grace. This letting go we experience mostly in a passive way for the first time, feeling it as being 'robbed', as a big loss; later on perhaps we are able to surrender the 'robbed thing', to give it to God freewillingly, and we can realise that then, paradoxically, the loss becomes a gain. Being robbed, letting go: diminishment in its full spiritual sense always is passive and active simultaneously.

God does not diminish us as a punishment or as an 'education', or because He is full of anger towards us sinners. If He diminishes us, it is to let us come nearer to Him, to make us more open for His grace to work in us. He must grow and we must be diminished.

One way seems to be that God tries (so often we resist!) to take away our ideals, first of all our pious ideals, to become a good Christian, to pray very well, and also to be very good in being diminished in becoming old and so on. But we have to live in God's reality, and that means that we are not very ideal. For Him that does not matter at all. We have to become as little and of no account as we really are, and in that state, let God love us. The older we become the more God wants us to live in His reality which is ours too, and not under the cloak of our wishes and fantasies.

One day my old age came into my room. That is a very funny story, for I am not very old at present. This old age was a small, very ancient and joyful person. She told me how she works. She said to me: I'll take away from you one thing after another, perhaps beginning with your teeth, your hair, looking young and fresh and so on. You have the choice. If you give me freewillingly what I want to have, I will bring it and give it to Christ as your gift; if you refuse, I will rob you of it, because I am much stronger than you, and put it in my own pocket! I was very amazed by this lesson, but it is a wonderful picture for our theme: Christ can be very creative in us when we are ready to be diminished, to let go our strength, our youth, all that we are, in becoming older and older. His challenges for obedience will grow - and the challenges to new creation within us.

Sister Anke SLG from 'The Creativity of Diminishment'

Although I do not hope to turn again
Although I do not hope
Although I do not hope to turn

Wavering between the profit and the loss
In this brief transit where the dreams cross
The dreamcrossed twilight between birth and dying
(Bless me father) though I do not wish to wish these things
From the wide window towards the granite shore
The white sails still fly seaward, seaward flying
Unbroken wings

And the lost heart stiffens and rejoices
In the lost lilac and the lost sea voices
And the weak spirit quickens to rebel
For the bent golden-rod and the lost sea smell
Quickens to recover
The cry of quail and the whirling plover
And the blind eye creates
The empty forms between the ivory gates
And smell renews the salt savour of the sandy earth

This is the time of tension between dying and birth
The place of solitude where three dreams cross
Between blue rocks
But when voices shaken from the yew tree drift away
Let the other yew be shaken and reply.

Blessèd sister, holy mother, spirit of the fountain, spirit of the garden,
Suffer us not to mock ourselves with falsehood
Teach us to care and not to care
Teach us to sit still
Even among these rocks,
Our peace in His will
And even among these rocks
Sister, mother
And the spirit of the river, spirit of the sea,
Suffer me not to be separated

And let my cry come unto Thee.

T S Eliot from 'Ash Wednesday VI'

NUNC DIMITTIS

The day fails; the darkness falls.
Now, O Lord my God,
Now let thy servant lay him down in peace;
For it is thou, Lord, only that makest him dwell in safety.

Out of my own night let me call, let me cry,
That I sleep not in sin unrepented.
Let my hands be clean, let my prayer be pure;
Let me look up to the brightness of thy glory,
With whom is no darkness at all.
Let my lying down be very trust, mine eyes close under thy blessing.
Let action sleep, and memory, and even thought; but not love,
Never my hope in Thee.
Into thy hands, O Lord, I commend my spirit.

While the body rests, quiet in thy keeping,
Let my soul ascend and sing in thy light:
Hosanna in the highest.

Eric Milner-White from 'My God, My Glory'

Heavenly Father,
    Stir our wills that we may obey you,
    Coax our minds that we understand you,
    Guide our hands that we may serve you,
    For in giving to others what we ourselves have been given,
        our true happiness will there be found.
                Amen

A prayer composed by Fr David

Opposite are extracts from the eulogy given by Reverend Bob Nichols at David's Funeral Service on the 26 October 2004 at Wymondham Abbey, Norfolk.

'On Thursday 14th October 2004 David Matheson Hunter died, aged 58. We rejoice at his gain; we weep at our loss.

When David was five, he was diagnosed as suffering from cystic fibrosis. David's life was *not* all about suffering: it was all about faith, hope and love, strong and sweet and shining, in the midst of suffering. Throughout his life, David *never* paraded that cross he had to bear.

David was a spiritual exemplar to all, with a lovely sense of humour and a seemingly endless capacity for making people feel special. His sermons were riveting and his devotional talks inspired all who listened. He was a true pastor - and a pastor to pastors.

What was visible to each and every one of us individually was David's overflowing love for his God and for his neighbour. In all that he did, but mostly in quiet moments away from the public eye, he encouraged and supported many, many people. He had time for everyone.

Let us pay tribute to David with our very lives. With his passing, the world has lost a powerful example of transforming faith, hope and love. May God free us and empower us worthily to follow David's example.'

Opposite are extracts from the address given by Mr Richard Hewitt, Lay Reader and Headmaster of Hartismere High School, Eye, Suffolk, at the Memorial Service held on the 12th December 2004 at St Andrew's Church, South Lopham.

'David Matheson Hunter BD AKC....scholar and academic....priest....historian........musician....actor....naturalist....artist....modelmaker....philosopher....sportsman. Good at them all, he enjoyed them all.

David.... the vast capacity for personal reflection....positive in all things, life's negatives twisted on their axes to take on meaningful form and to yield a fruitful experience... determination, sometimes with a deal of obstinacy, sometimes with great compassion, nearly always with an unworldly, unconstrained sense of time....

Cystic Fibrosis....the record years of a full and luminous light....years of action, song, drama, laughter and achievement....a soul commissioned to God.

David opened many doors, far more than he closed....he would tell us that God gives strength to those who test their own capacities to the full...that each of us has at least one unique gift, a skill, a smile, a way of thinking, to share with the rest...he would tell us to support and value each other...to uphold the standards in which we believe.

Think of David saying the words of the Hymn of Thanksgiving from Isaiah: "God is my Saviour, I will trust him and not be afraid. The Lord gives me power and strength. As fresh water brings joy to the thirsty, so God's people rejoice when he saves them." May we, every one of us, share in that rejoicing with David.'

ACKNOWLEDGEMENTS

Thanks is expressed to the following for their kind permission to reproduce material of which they are the publishers, authors, or copyright owners.

Arthur James Ltd, a prayer by William Portsmouth from *Healing Prayer* (p.40); © copyright Burns & Oates, a Continuum imprint, used by permission of the Continuum International Publishing Group Ltd for an extract from *The Icon* by Michael Quenot (p.25); Burrswood, Groombridge, for Dorothy Kerin's 'A Little Way of Prayer' from *Chapel House Notes* 1936 (p.17); Dover Publications for 'Christ and the Soldier' from *War Poems* by Siegfried Sassoon (pp. 30,31); Faber & Faber Ltd for an extract by Dag Hammarskjold from *Markings* (p.43), and for extracts by T S Eliot from *Four Quartets: Burnt Norton* (p.36), *East Coker* (p.42), and from T S Eliot's *Ash Wednesday* (pp. 56, 57); HarperCollins Publishers Australia for two poems by Michael Leunig from *A Common Prayer* (pp. 23 & 25); 'Not All There' from *The Poetry of Robert Frost* edited by Edward Connery Lathem, Copyright 1936 by Robert Frost, Copyright 1964 by Lesley Frost Ballantine, © 1969 by Henry Holt and Company, Reprinted by permission of Henry Holt and Company, LLC (p.28); for an extract by C S Lewis © C S Lewis Pte Ltd (p.26); Sisters of the Love of God © SLG Press 1990 for an extract from *The Creativity of Diminishment* by Sister Anke (pp. 54, 55); SPCK for prayers from *My God, My Glory* by E Milner-White (pp. 8 & 58); Sun Chalice Books for extracts from *The Lord of the Dance* by Anthony Duncan (p. 9).

Every effort has been made to trace the original source of copyright material in this anthology, but where this has not been found, I offer my sincere apologies - Hilary Hunter, widow of the compiler.